Becoming me....

Nisha Nair

Presentation by *BookLeaf Publishing*

Web: www.bookleafpub.com

E-mail: info@bookleafpub.com

ISBN: 9789357214223

First edition 2023

*To all who have come and gone and has helped
me in becoming me*

ACKNOWLEDGEMENT

For all those who has let go of hatred

who treats all beings with kindness

and compassion, who is always calm and peaceful, unmoved by pain or pleasure,

free of the "I" and "mine," - Bhagavad-Gita

PREFACE

Becoming me is a collection of poems that will take you for a ride through ups and downs of life and gives an insight into making the best within the means we have.. The book makes us believe in the wider good, and talks about goodness that still prevails and unexplored.

Pause a while, let me know you more..

In a spur of a moment, I catch a glipmse
Of little wonders that maketh the life
Be a fly, a bee or a bird
Be a child, an young or an old
A car that speeds, or a cycle that rolls
With no regard, rushing past,
In a bubble, not made to last

Nobody cares, what goes around
Nobody dares to pause for a while
To give a glance and pass a smile
Slow down my world....
There's more to life than to chase
There's more to us, that we should know
The atoms, molecules and cells
Together we are spun....
In a cosmic realm of the universe
We are all but one...

The life that flows in you and me
Every breathe we take and leave
That's the life force that goes from me
That's the life force that comes to you
I cannot think to walk the world

Without the vital source that I tap from you
Our souls are entwined in a mystic way
So pause a while, let me know you more....

My one line story....

There s a little story i tell myself
To no one else , but to myself
In this story, I am the best,
No matter how vulnerable and fearful I am
This story leads me through the toughest times
In my bestest and worst dream, I am always the
best..

In this story , I am a child , i never grow
This inner child is always strong
I peep out through my inner self
In search of a familiar scene , a familiar voice or
a face
This child sees nothing familiar, to its dismay...
Yet, moves on picking the trails
Adding it to the story, and shaping it to the best..

This little story makes me sob
 i change plots, chisel and level it
But it always remains a story with the one line
phrase
That i am the best....

This one story is the only truth
I know of myself

I keep it together , making a vow to myself ,
never to fail
Coz, in my story, I am the best
And to lose would be the deadliest blow

Dont we all tell a story to ourselves ?
That one punch line story ...
That drives you to live
That makes you laugh and cry..
That one story thats never fails
Never disappointments , never abandons
Follows like a shadow
Rings in your ears until it becomes your inner
story
That shapes the whole you..
And hatches a scheme
so that you never ever lose...

Narrow Road Unto Happiness..

Loneliness is nothing, but a state of mind,
Look inside, to find a world, so kind...
Very lesson of love, is to love yourself
When you lose it, we dread ourselves Thousands
surround you, still it aches
 Happiness is, when you live for your sake...

Loneliness is nothing, but a state of mind
Look inside, to find a world, so kind...
The race is lost, when the purpose is lost,
 Find your thrust, to live at the most.
The life gives chances, to make your best
Success favors those who pursue thier quest...

Loneliness is nothing, but a state of mind
Look inside, to find a world, so kind...
Keep your pace, love the journey
Don't be fret, just push your boundary
You will know it, when you get there ,
But life will sting, if you don't share..

Soul Child..

Deep inside me, resides a soul child
Waiting to be born, to live a life king size
The child in me cries..
shuddering at the rustle of a leaf
Fear grips, darkness frightens
Hiding behind the shadow, my soul wails
Standing unsure of my path
Obscured by my mental pain

And one day a wind comes
I get swept by its fierce force
Blewing me across the tall spire
So high I went, the wind shook me hard
I shed the weight of my sorrows and fear..
Sky clears, I see my sun
As the fog fades, the wind and sun embrace
And I am reborn as their soul child..

The story called We

When am sure, where to head...
I move in a haste, with the end in sight
Failing to notice the smaller bits
That garnered to become the larger whole
I might have gone so far,
But to dismay, I failed to know
The journey to it was the real truth
The roads i walked was the real goal
The faces i met, friendships i forged
The people who helped,
The daily rituals i did, from dawn to dusk
Are the real treasures, i picked on our way
That gets connected, to the story called WE

A Flickering moment

We have so many reasons to smile
than we think we have…
When I wake up to a sunny day
I live in the present…
A present…
That was my future, an instant ago

If I don't love this moment,
Why did I crave for it with all my heart?
Every moment is a longing from our past
It was here we are striving to reach
But my woe, as we get there,
we instantly dream of the next

Give me a little time my flickering mind
 Let me drench in this moment, nothing more I
ask..
Before my heart would yearn for another
moment from future
That's just a promise of a time that's yet to
come..
Let me just bask in the beauty of this time….

We are not yet lost..

This lush greenery that's abound
The trees, birds and the winding paths
A reminder of goodness still prevails
When we say, the world is wicked
When we say, we forgot our roots
When we say, we are chic and modern
Deep beneath lies an ocean of kindness
Still awaiting to explode..

The belief that we are still bonded
Is the oneness of our being
We are not yet lost..
Can we walk back to the crossroad?
Where we took the wrong turn..

An Ode to the spring

Spring is here in its full bloom
But all that seen is a painful gloom
The nature has flowered, but for whom?
Is the world, pushed to a doom?

But our history is to fight it back
Epidemic, recession we will sack
And chase the virus with a whack
The world will come back to track

Sun will rise, in all its shine
Our efforts will not, go in drain
We cannot sit back and simply whine
Do your part and leave rest to divine

The nature is scarred, with dirt and grime
Let us flush it, down the drain
In all its grandeur, spring will come,
The world will thrive, on its own.

When we know the price of nature
We will learn how to care and nurture
Better, lets not muddle with its features
The world belong to all its creatures.

To be a cloud..

What it gives to be a cloud ..
To be unbound, fluffy and white
A great smile perhaps ,
That smile that knows nothing
Absolutely nothing...
Just a placid plain smile
Then you become a cloud
Feeling so light and so bright....

What it gives to be a cloud?
Airy and buoyant..
As the wind sweeps off your feet..
You shed the weight of unrequited love
Burden of a life time..
The love that never saw the light of the day..
Carried within your uncared being..
Like the clouds that gets rid of its plight..
On the hardened earth...
For the clouds, its unfathomable pain..
But for the earth , its hope of life...

Like the clouds...
Today I feel light..
I have shed my weight
That have held me tight

Am unbound, fluffy and white
My smile, says it all..

Becoming me

Becoming me was tough
Sailing through the worst times
But holding to my dreams tight
Unwavering in the face of untold ordeals
Swimming across the waves
Sometimes with it, sometimes across
Or just lying flat
So the strong undercurrents can pass..
In a frantic urge to reach my shore
That i have just seen from afar..
Finally, when i became me,
i lost me, in whole...

The Fall

The fall from the heights to death
Unto the eternity
Before the last breathe you heaved
For the last time, your heart skipped to beat
What crossed your mind, was it us ?

On that rainy dark night
When you laid frozen and numb
And your bones broken to bits
The wind that passed
Would have soothed you
The rain would have sung a song

That fall from heights to death
Would have been painful
When you let go ,
Your hands would have wanted to grab
The last straw of hope
You would have known
That was your last .....
A small tear would have fallen
You would have cried, the last cry
Those last tears would have kept you warm

I can now be at peace
I no more suffer in your sufferings
From the pain you endured
I am at peace , the rain and wind
And the warm tears make me calm
The last companions that helped you pass
To another realm , i know you will never return
Before you go , for the last time
Turn your face , let me etch that in my heart...

When the sun has gone...

When the sun has gone
And its last golden ray turned grey
The wrinkled sky is frozen
And the dreams lay broken

When the sun was here
I could not reap its shine
Its rays turned grey
And the light went out
Time stood still, numbed and bare

The sun has gone,
its rays have withdrawn
But dreams lay shattered ,
Its my loss, I can never harness them back

Make your life ..
When the sun is shining..
Time is short..
Makes the best of the gleaming light
While you are still here..
All alive and more ..

Never Belonged...

There are people around
Their noises, I don't recognize
I can sit alone away from the pandemonium
All alone, completely lost in my world
Shrinking to my own being,
Keeping the door to my soul
All closed and tight..

People fear me, I am scared of small talks
I can never belong
Rather prefer to walk alone , to sink in to my
dreams
Where no one can know my inner thoughts
The turmoils that I go through ,
I am encompassed by a blissful feelings of
solitude
Pain or ecstacy, is all mine to know

I can never belong
People tire me,
Rather I would burrow in my deep thoughts
Talking to my alter being..
It makes more sense

I can never belong
People freak me ,
I admire them but I can never be them..
But give me a day with someone
Who can admire the beauty of my being
Just that someone, if not more
Because that would be the day
I would really belong.......

The child that was lost....

Sorry child, I could not find you
Your childhood was snatched.
The sweetness of being a child was robbed
Years did pass , you did grow
As a lost adult searching for the strayed
childhood
It puzzles me..
Are you a child or an adult?
Or a child trapped in an adult being
Who craves for a lullaby
The amusements and happiness
To chase behind the dragonfly
To feel light as a butterfly
I can give a lifetime
Once more, if i can be that child who was lost

To live one more day...

Living with the feeling
Of being an outcast
Failing every move,
Failing the love
Failed everything that came my way..

I want to live for more day..
Where I will vanquish the deeds I failed
Love, relations and my soul..
To appease the wailing,
To silence the cries..
For no one knows..
What lies beneath
There is an ocean of love unexplored
Feats that was never won..
Let me put myself together
And live for one more day..
Where winning streak will be my crown..

I feel all so light..

It snowed, much to my delight
Whites every where, cold and bright
I sat by the window , looking at the flakes
And i felt, all so light...
Soothing my senses in a gentlest way..
The harsh cold, spoke of beauty..
Like a song, that's long forgotten..
Of memories that's hard to recollect..
That lay frozen, yearning to come alive..
The more you strived, the more it sinked.
In to the whiteness, cold and damp..

As the flakes hits the ground
And vanished like a forgotten dream..
I stayed there for a bit...
For me it was a cue,
To undo me and start again..
And shed the years of pain
Thats never resolved..
Those memories
That's hard to unearth..
Like the barrenness of the bitter cold...

And it snowed , much to delight
And I felt, all so light..

Song of a leaf..

When autumn is here...
Winter can't be afar
As the chilly wind blows..
A lone leaf wait to fall.
It just hesitates, clings to life
Nothing can stand the stirring force..
It did fall , with a heavy heart..
The earth welcomed the leaf..
No matter, how withered it was..
The leaf is entwined in its soul,
Waiting for another spring..
Spring can be far, but time shall pass
When the seeds are scattered on the earth's lap
That's enriched with soul of the lone leaf..
The leaf gave itself, a new life sprouts...

That was never the real me..

I tried to be my best self
Amidst the chaos the life threw
But my heart got sealed, the lock is lost..
Where it can be?

My "best self" is the one
That laughs at the silliest jokes
Coz, you don't have to think
But be the stupidest version of you

My soul is disposed,
It's not me you see
Its the moulded form of me
That don't think , but just laughs
Coz , the world needs people who are blind
Follow the lot,
But have no mind on its own

I tried to let go of the silly me
But I get shunned, the moment I set loose
Sorry world, the one that smiles
It's not my best self..
I will be my best
The day I decide to walk away..
The day I would find the key to my heart

That would set me free..
From the bonds that tether me
To an unknown sense of self ..
A hypocritical, blown out version.
That was never the real me...

9 789357 214223